LEGO® *Star Wars*®
MAD LIBS

concept created by Roger Price & Leonard Stern

PSS!

PRICE STERN SLOAN
An Imprint of Penguin Group (USA) Inc.

PRICE STERN SLOAN
Published by the Penguin Group
Penguin Group (USA) Inc., 375 Hudson Street, New York, New York 10014, USA
Penguin Group (Canada), 90 Eglinton Avenue East, Suite 700,
Toronto, Ontario M4P 2Y3, Canada
(a division of Pearson Penguin Canada Inc.)
Penguin Books Ltd., 80 Strand, London WC2R 0RL, England
Penguin Group Ireland, 25 St. Stephen's Green, Dublin 2, Ireland
(a division of Penguin Books Ltd.)
Penguin Group (Australia), 250 Camberwell Road, Camberwell, Victoria 3124, Australia
(a division of Pearson Australia Group Pty. Ltd.)
Penguin Books India Pvt. Ltd., 11 Community Centre,
Panchsheel Park, New Delhi—110 017, India
Penguin Group (NZ), 67 Apollo Drive, Rosedale, Auckland 0632, New Zealand
(a division of Pearson New Zealand Ltd.)
Penguin Books (South Africa) (Pty.) Ltd., 24 Sturdee Avenue,
Rosebank, Johannesburg 2196, South Africa

Penguin Books Ltd., Registered Offices:
80 Strand, London WC2R 0RL, England

Published by Price Stern Sloan, a division of Penguin Young Readers Group,
345 Hudson Street, New York, New York 10014.

ISBN 978-0-8431-7025-2

3 5 7 9 10 8 6 4

MAD LIBS

INSTRUCTIONS

MAD LIBS® is a game for people who don't like games!
It can be played by one, two, three, four, or forty.

• RIDICULOUSLY SIMPLE DIRECTIONS

In this tablet you will find stories containing blank spaces where words
are left out. One player, the READER, selects one of these stories. The
READER does not tell anyone what the story is about. Instead, he/she asks
the other players, the WRITERS, to give him/her words. These words are
used to fill in the blank spaces in the story.

• TO PLAY

The READER asks each WRITER in turn to call out words—an adjective
or a noun or whatever the space calls for—and uses them to fill in the blank
spaces in the story. The result is a MAD LIBS® game.

When the READER then reads the completed MAD LIBS® game to the
other players, they will discover that they have written a story that is
fantastic, screamingly funny, shocking, silly, crazy, or just plain dumb—
depending upon which words each WRITER called out.

• EXAMPLE (*Before* and *After*)

" _____ !" he said _____
       EXCLAMATION   ADVERB

as he jumped into his convertible _____ and
                                     NOUN

drove off with his _____ wife.
                   ADJECTIVE

" *Ouch* !" he said *Stupidly*
       EXCLAMATION   ADVERB

as he jumped into his convertible *cat* and
                                       NOUN

drove off with his *brave* wife.
                   ADJECTIVE

MAD LIBS

QUICK REVIEW

In case you have forgotten what adjectives, adverbs, nouns, and verbs are, here is a quick review:

An ADJECTIVE describes something or somebody. *Lumpy*, *soft*, *ugly*, *messy*, and *short* are adjectives.

An ADVERB tells how something is done. It modifies a verb and usually ends in "ly." *Modestly*, *stupidly*, *greedily*, and *carefully* are adverbs.

A NOUN is the name of a person, place, or thing. *Sidewalk*, *umbrella*, *bridle*, *bathtub*, and *nose* are nouns.

A VERB is an action word. *Run*, *pitch*, *jump*, and *swim* are verbs. Put the verbs in past tense if the directions say PAST TENSE. *Ran*, *pitched*, *jumped*, and *swam* are verbs in the past tense.

When we ask for A PLACE, we mean any sort of place: a country or city (*Spain*, *Cleveland*) or a room (*bathroom*, *kitchen*).

An EXCLAMATION or SILLY WORD is any sort of funny sound, gasp, grunt, or outcry, like *Wow!*, *Ouch!*, *Whomp!*, *Ick!*, and *Gadzooks!*

When we ask for specific words, like a NUMBER, a COLOR, an ANIMAL, or a PART OF THE BODY, we mean a word that is one of those things, like *seven*, *blue*, *horse*, or *head*.

When we ask for a PLURAL, it means more than one. For example, *cat* pluralized is *cats*.

MAD LIBS® is fun to play with friends, but you can also play it by yourself! To begin with, DO NOT look at the story on the page below. Fill in the blanks on this page with the words called for. Then, using the words you have selected, fill in the blank spaces in the story.

Now you've created your own hilarious MAD LIBS® game!

LEGO® *STAR WARS*®

ADJECTIVE _____

NOUN _____

NOUN _____

NOUN _____

NOUN _____

VERB _____

ADJECTIVE _____

NOUN _____

NOUN _____

ADJECTIVE _____

PERSON IN ROOM _____

PLURAL NOUN _____

NOUN _____

MAD LIBS

LEGO® STAR WARS®

A/An ___stinky___ time ago, in a/an ___stuffed crust pizza___
ADJECTIVE   NOUN

far, far away.... It is a period of civil ___War___. Rebel
NOUN

spaceships, striking from a hidden ___bathroom___, have won
NOUN

their first victory against the evil Galactic ___Kitty___.
NOUN

During the battle, Rebel spies managed to ___eat___
VERB

secret plans to the Empire's ___Stimy___ weapon, the Death
ADJECTIVE

___Fart___, an armored space station with enough power
NOUN

to destroy an entire ___universe___. Pursued by the Empire's
NOUN

___dumb___ agents, Princess ___Bob___ races home
ADJECTIVE   PERSON IN ROOM

aboard her starship, custodian of the stolen ___cats___ that
PLURAL NOUN

can save her people and restore ___noise___ to the galaxy . . .
NOUN

MAD LIBS® is fun to play with friends, but you can also play it by yourself! To begin with, DO NOT look at the story on the page below. Fill in the blanks on this page with the words called for. Then, using the words you have selected, fill in the blank spaces in the story.

Now you've created your own hilarious MAD LIBS® game!

PROTOCOL DROID SALES PITCH, TRANSLATED FROM JAWA TRADE LANGUAGE

VERB _____

ADJECTIVE _____

NOUN _____

PLURAL NOUN _____

NUMBER _____

PLURAL NOUN _____

PLURAL NOUN _____

ADJECTIVE _____

COLOR _____

ADJECTIVE _____

NOUN _____

OCCUPATION _____

NOUN _____

ADJECTIVE _____

NOUN _____

VERB _____

MAD LIBS®
PROTOCOL DROID SALES PITCH,
TRANSLATED FROM JAWA
TRADE LANGUAGE

Although some people might prefer to __Eat__
VERB

a brand-new droid, used protocol droids always make for a/an

__Furry__ purchase. This droid __animal thing__ was
ADJECTIVE   NOUN

designed to interact with __cats__ and translate over
PLURAL NOUN

__1,11,11,111__ languages and forms of communication, and he has
NUMBER

been conditioned to specifically address matters of __turds__
PLURAL NOUN

and __toys__. Yes, his circuitry may be __rusty__,
PLURAL NOUN   ADJECTIVE

but his __purple__ plating has been refurbished and he
COLOR

has proven himself sturdy and __stinky__ in assisting his
ADJECTIVE

previous owners. In fact, this particular __thingie__ has served
NOUN

many diplomatic masters, including Galactic Senators, royalty, and

even a/an __cleaning job__! He also seems to get along well with
OCCUPATION

a well-known R2 unit, so if you'd like both, I can make you a/an

__animal__. Just a warning, though: He seems to be a bit
NOUN

nervous about __smelly__ travel, so before you take off in your
ADJECTIVE

__bathroom__, you might want to __tape__ him down.
NOUN   VERB

MAD LIBS® is fun to play with friends, but you can also play it by yourself! To begin with, DO NOT look at the story on the page below. Fill in the blanks on this page with the words called for. Then, using the words you have selected, fill in the blank spaces in the story.

Now you've created your own hilarious MAD LIBS® game!

JEDI TRAINING DIARY, BY YODA

ADJECTIVE _____

PERSON IN ROOM _____

NOUN _____

ADJECTIVE _____

ADJECTIVE _____

SAME PERSON IN ROOM _____

NOUN _____

NOUN _____

NOUN _____

VERB _____

TYPE OF LIQUID _____

NOUN _____

LAST NAME _____

MAD LIBS®
JEDI TRAINING DIARY, BY YODA

Learning I am if this new Padawan is ready to be a/an __Smelly__
                                                          ADJECTIVE

Jedi. __Nolan__ has shown talent with the Force, but
          PERSON IN ROOM

__toilet__, he/she seems to be lacking. A Jedi warrior
   NOUN

should not forget where they leave their __stinky__
                                                 ADJECTIVE

lightsaber, no matter how __fun__ they were training
                                 ADJECTIVE

the night before. __Nolan__ was not able to use the
                        SAME PERSON IN ROOM

__bathroom__ to lift an X-wing __Kitty__ out of the
 NOUN   NOUN

__fire__ yesterday, even when I said to __poop__
  NOUN   VERB

harder. And being dropped into the swampy __Hawian Punch__
                                            TYPE OF LIQUID

I do not like, when a Padawan forgets to fasten the buckles on his

__Cat__ before doing backflips. The Force tells me there
  NOUN

is another __Saloedo__, but take my chances with that one,
         LAST NAME

I think I will not!

MAD LIBS® is fun to play with friends, but you can also play it by yourself! To begin with, DO NOT look at the story on the page below. Fill in the blanks on this page with the words called for. Then, using the words you have selected, fill in the blank spaces in the story.

Now you've created your own hilarious MAD LIBS® game!

SELECTING A BOUNTY HUNTER, BY JABBA THE HUTT

PART OF THE BODY _____

ADJECTIVE _____

VERB _____

ADJECTIVE _____

VERB _____

NOUN _____

NOUN _____

NOUN _____

PART OF THE BODY _____

PART OF THE BODY (PLURAL) _____

NUMBER _____

NOUN _____

MAD LIBS
SELECTING A BOUNTY HUNTER, BY JABBA THE HUTT

There are several things to keep in _____ when
PART OF THE BODY
you need to hire a bounty hunter. First of all, bounty hunters are

notoriously _____ , so they might not even show
ADJECTIVE
up when you _____ them. Some are cunning and
VERB

_____ , while others are ruthless and would rather just
ADJECTIVE
walk up and _____ their target. Consider their choice
VERB
of weapon, too. Just because someone walks in with the biggest

_____ doesn't mean they know how to use it. You
NOUN
will need to take into account what the bounty _____ looks
NOUN
like as well. Some are human and may wear a/an _____ over
NOUN
their _____ to blend in. Others might have webbed
PART OF THE BODY
_____ . Also, if you choose to hire a droid, make
PART OF THE BODY (PLURAL)
sure it isn't _____ feet tall, or it might not even fit
NUMBER
through the front _____ !
NOUN

MAD LIBS® is fun to play with friends, but you can also play it by yourself! To begin with, DO NOT look at the story on the page below. Fill in the blanks on this page with the words called for. Then, using the words you have selected, fill in the blank spaces in the story.

Now you've created your own hilarious MAD LIBS® game!

BUILDING THE PERFECT DEATH STAR

NOUN _____

ADJECTIVE _____

NOUN _____

ADJECTIVE _____

NUMBER _____

PLURAL NOUN _____

NUMBER _____

ADJECTIVE _____

PLURAL NOUN _____

NOUN _____

ADJECTIVE _____

NOUN _____

NOUN _____

NOUN _____

MAD LIBS®
BUILDING THE PERFECT
DEATH STAR

When your Empire is trying to rule an entire _____,

                                                NOUN

having a/an _____ space station like the Death Star can

             ADJECTIVE

come in handy. It should be the size of a small _____.

                                              NOUN

At the very least, it should be _____ enough to hold

                                ADJECTIVE

at least _____ stormtroopers and have a docking

                 NUMBER

area where pilots can take off and land their _____.

                                        PLURAL NOUN

Because there are over _____ people living on board,

                            NUMBER

you will need a/an _____ compactor to handle all of the

                          ADJECTIVE

_____ that is generated each day. You will need holding

PLURAL NOUN

cells in case you capture a princess and you suspect her of being a/an

_____. Most importantly, you will need to have a large

         NOUN

_____ beam, which should be capable of destroying

        ADJECTIVE

a planet with a single _____. Just be sure that your

                          NOUN

reactor core _____ isn't exposed in case someone decides

                NOUN

to fire a photon _____ in that direction!

              NOUN

MAD LIBS® is fun to play with friends, but you can also play it by yourself! To begin with, DO NOT look at the story on the page below. Fill in the blanks on this page with the words called for. Then, using the words you have selected, fill in the blank spaces in the story.

Now you've created your own hilarious MAD LIBS® game!

THE PERILS OF INTERGALACTIC PRINCESSHOOD

NOUN _____

NOUN _____

ADJECTIVE _____

PLURAL NOUN _____

PLURAL NOUN _____

ADJECTIVE _____

NOUN _____

VERB _____

ADJECTIVE _____

NOUN _____

NOUN _____

PART OF THE BODY (PLURAL) _____

PART OF THE BODY _____

MAD LIBS
THE PERILS OF INTERGALACTIC PRINCESSHOOD

Being a princess can sometimes be a challenge. You might be

asked to go on a diplomatic _____ on behalf of your
                                    NOUN

_____, only for Imperial forces to intercept your ship
       NOUN

and accuse you of working with the _____ forces. You
                                          ADJECTIVE

will probably have to associate with all kinds of _____—
                                                      PLURAL NOUN

they could be old _____, _____ smugglers,
                      PLURAL NOUN   ADJECTIVE

or even a Wookiee. You should probably learn how to use a/an

_____ for your own protection, and you might even
       NOUN

need to _____ a speeder bike, which can be tricky on a/an
            VERB

_____ planet like Endor. Just one suggestion: If you
    ADJECTIVE

want to be prepared for whatever _____ you encounter,
                                        NOUN

it is best to be ready for action at all times. In order to see what's

coming, be sure to keep your _____ out of your
                                    NOUN

_____. You might want to consider wearing braids
PART OF THE BODY (PLURAL)

or buns in your _____!
                    PART OF THE BODY

MAD LIBS® is fun to play with friends, but you can also play it by yourself! To begin with, DO NOT look at the story on the page below. Fill in the blanks on this page with the words called for. Then, using the words you have selected, fill in the blank spaces in the story.

Now you've created your own hilarious MAD LIBS® game!

PILOTING
THE MILLENNIUM FALCON

NOUN _____

ADJECTIVE _____

NOUN _____

ADJECTIVE _____

PLURAL NOUN_____

PLURAL NOUN _____

NOUN _____

ADJECTIVE _____

NOUN _____

PLURAL NOUN _____

PLURAL NOUN _____

NOUN _____

NOUN _____

NOUN _____

SILLY WORD _____

MAD LIBS®
PILOTING
THE MILLENNIUM FALCON

The *Millennium* _____ might not look like much
NOUN

to the _____ observer, but what appears to be a
ADJECTIVE

hunk of _____ is actually a very _____
NOUN   ADJECTIVE

ship. It can fly faster than the speed of _____—in
PLURAL NOUN

fact, it's been known to make the Kessel Run in less than twelve

_____. With its navigational _____ and a/an
PLURAL NOUN   NOUN

_____ copilot, it is even capable of traveling through
ADJECTIVE

hyper-_____. In addition, the ship has been modified
NOUN

so that it is perfect for smuggling contraband _____.
PLURAL NOUN

And should you wind up in an unexpected battle with some Imperial

_____, you can activate the _____ generator
PLURAL NOUN   NOUN

and fire the twin blasters or the hidden laser _____. Of
NOUN

course, there might be some downtime, too, so feel free to play games

on the holographic _____. Just don't wager too much in
NOUN

a game of _____—that's how the last owner lost this ship!
SILLY WORD

MAD LIBS® is fun to play with friends, but you can also play it by yourself! To begin with, DO NOT look at the story on the page below. Fill in the blanks on this page with the words called for. Then, using the words you have selected, fill in the blank spaces in the story.

Now you've created your own hilarious MAD LIBS® game!

PODRACING PODCAST

ADJECTIVE _____

NOUN _____

SILLY WORD _____

NOUN _____

VERB _____

NUMBER _____

NOUN _____

PLURAL NOUN _____

PLURAL NOUN _____

VERB _____

NOUN _____

VERB _____

ADJECTIVE _____

NOUN _____

NOUN _____

MAD LIBS
PODRACING PODCAST

Welcome to today's _____ Podrace! And have
ADJECTIVE

we got a/an _____ for you! Today, here at Mos
NOUN

_____ Raceway, we actually have a/an _____
SILLY WORD   NOUN

who will be competing! Can you believe that? His name is Anakin

Sky-_____-er, and he is apparently only _____
VERB   NUMBER

years old. And they're off! The racers are speeding around the

_____. Some of the racers seem to be having trouble
NOUN

with their _____. In fact, several of them have already
PLURAL NOUN

crashed into the _____. And now we have some Tusken
PLURAL NOUN

Raiders, who have decided to _____ at the racers! At
VERB

this point, it seems to be a two-_____ race. The first
NOUN

racer is trying to cut off Sky-_____-er, but now their
VERB

_____ rods have become tangled! It looks like the
ADJECTIVE

human is pulling away, and smoke is pouring out of the other driver's

_____! Unbelievable—who would have thought that a
NOUN

human _____ could win!
NOUN

MAD LIBS® is fun to play with friends, but you can also play it by yourself! To begin with, DO NOT look at the story on the page below. Fill in the blanks on this page with the words called for. Then, using the words you have selected, fill in the blank spaces in the story.

Now you've created your own hilarious MAD LIBS® game!

WANTED: DARTH MAUL

ADJECTIVE _____

NOUN _____

ADJECTIVE _____

PLURAL NOUN _____

COLOR _____

COLOR _____

PLURAL NOUN _____

PART OF THE BODY _____

ARTICLE OF CLOTHING _____

SILLY WORD _____

ADJECTIVE _____

ADVERB _____

NOUN _____

NOUN _____

NUMBER _____

ADJECTIVE _____

NOUN _____

MAD LIBS®
WANTED: DARTH MAUL

All Jedi should be on the lookout for a/an _____
                                              ADJECTIVE

Sith Lord known as Darth Maul. He has been trained as a/an

_____ by Darth Sidious and is strong in the _____
      NOUN   ADJECTIVE

side of the Force. As a Sith, he has _____ all over his body,
                                          PLURAL NOUN

including his face, which is demonically decorated in _____
                                                           COLOR

and _____. Darth Maul also has _____ sticking
         COLOR   PLURAL NOUN

out of the top of his _____. He wears a black
                          PART OF THE BODY

_____ and has been trained in many forms of
   ARTICLE OF CLOTHING

combat, including the martial arts of _____. He is very
                                           SILLY WORD

_____ and is able to move very _____ to
    ADJECTIVE   ADVERB

disarm or injure his _____ in battle. He also wields a
                          NOUN

special light-_____ that has _____ blades,
                NOUN   NUMBER

making him even more _____. If any Jedi should see
                          ADJECTIVE

Darth Maul, be advised to use caution in approaching him—or better

yet, wait for another _____ to arrive!
                          NOUN

MAD LIBS® is fun to play with friends, but you can also play it by yourself! To begin with, DO NOT look at the story on the page below. Fill in the blanks on this page with the words called for. Then, using the words you have selected, fill in the blank spaces in the story.

Now you've created your own hilarious MAD LIBS® game!

THE WINTRY
PLANET OF HOTH

NOUN _____

ADJECTIVE _____

NUMBER _____

VERB _____

NOUN _____

PLURAL NOUN _____

PLURAL NOUN _____

ADJECTIVE _____

ADJECTIVE _____

NOUN _____

ADJECTIVE _____

NOUN _____

TYPE OF LIQUID _____

MAD LIBS®
THE WINTRY PLANET OF HOTH

Looking for a cool _____ for your next vacation? Well,
NOUN

consider visiting the ice planet of Hoth! Perfect for when you're

looking to escape the _____ heat of a home planet with
ADJECTIVE

_____ suns, Hoth's temperatures rarely _____
NUMBER   VERB

above freezing. Tired of dealing with an overcrowded, bustling

_____ like Mos Eisley? You won't find many
NOUN

_____ of scum or villainy here—in fact, no human
PLURAL NOUN

_____ are known to live here at all! You might run into the
PLURAL NOUN

occasional tauntaun, but they tend to have a very _____
ADJECTIVE

disposition. In fact, you can even ride them, and they'll also help keep

you _____ at night. But if you hear a wampa howling,
ADJECTIVE

watch out! If one of those furry creatures finds you when it's in need

of a good _____, you might end up going back to its
NOUN

place for dinner—as the _____ course! As far as getting
ADJECTIVE

around, any sort of _____ should be fine as long as you
NOUN

make sure the _____ doesn't freeze in the tank!
TYPE OF LIQUID

MAD LIBS® is fun to play with friends, but you can also play it by yourself! To begin with, DO NOT look at the story on the page below. Fill in the blanks on this page with the words called for. Then, using the words you have selected, fill in the blank spaces in the story.

Now you've created your own hilarious MAD LIBS® game!

HAN SOLO'S
SPACEBOOK PROFILE

NOUN _____

OCCUPATION _____

NOUN _____

NOUN _____

NOUN _____

PERSON IN ROOM _____

SILLY WORD _____

PLURAL NOUN _____

NOUN _____

ADJECTIVE _____

ADJECTIVE _____

ADJECTIVE _____

NOUN _____

VERB _____

MAD LIBS
HAN SOLO'S
SPACEBOOK PROFILE

Name: Han Solo

Occupation: _____ Smuggler, Rebel _____, Scoundrel
            NOUN   OCCUPATION

Former Business Associates: Jabba the _____
                                           NOUN

Lives in: My ship, the *Millennium* _____
                                    NOUN

_____ Status: It's complicated with Princess _____
NOUN   PERSON IN ROOM

Hobbies: Playing games like sabacc and _____
                                         SILLY WORD

_____ Spoken: English, Wookiee, Huttese
PLURAL NOUN

Dislikes: _____ Hunters, Commitment
             NOUN

Favorite Quotes:

"I've got a/an _____ feeling about this."
                   ADJECTIVE

"_____ religions and _____ weapons are
       ADJECTIVE   ADJECTIVE

no match for a good _____ at your side."
                       NOUN

"_____ it up, fuzz ball!"
     VERB

MAD LIBS® is fun to play with friends, but you can also play it by yourself! To begin with, DO NOT look at the story on the page below. Fill in the blanks on this page with the words called for. Then, using the words you have selected, fill in the blank spaces in the story.

Now you've created your own hilarious MAD LIBS® game!

CARBON FREEZING

SILLY WORD _____

PLURAL NOUN _____

ADJECTIVE _____

ADJECTIVE _____

NOUN _____

NOUN _____

NOUN _____

NOUN _____

NOUN _____

NOUN _____

NOUN _____

PART OF THE BODY _____

PART OF THE BODY (PLURAL) _____

ADJECTIVE _____

PART OF THE BODY _____

MAD LIBS®
CARBON FREEZING

If you ever try to double-cross an intergalactic gangster like

_____ the Hutt, you might end up encased in
    SILLY WORD

_____. The process really isn't very _____.
    PLURAL NOUN   ADJECTIVE

You will find yourself lowered into a/an _____ chamber,
                                          ADJECTIVE

where you are then frozen inside a large block of _____.
                                           NOUN

After that, you could end up hanging on someone's _____
                                           NOUN

or even used as a piece of furniture, such as a/an _____.
                                           NOUN

However, you don't need to worry about that as you won't feel

a/an _____. If you are eventually released from your
             NOUN

suspended _____, you might experience _____
             NOUN   NOUN

sickness, provided you survive the _____. You
                                  NOUN

could feel numbness or stiffness in your _____, and
                                    PART OF THE BODY

your _____ might take some time to get
        PART OF THE BODY (PLURAL)

back to normal. But the most important thing to remember is,

when you're frozen, try to smile so you won't be stuck with a/an

_____ look on your _____!
    ADJECTIVE   PART OF THE BODY

MAD LIBS® is fun to play with friends, but you can also play it by yourself! To begin with, DO NOT look at the story on the page below. Fill in the blanks on this page with the words called for. Then, using the words you have selected, fill in the blank spaces in the story.

Now you've created your own hilarious MAD LIBS® game!

THE EWOKS OF ENDOR

PLURAL NOUN _____

NUMBER _____

COLOR _____

PLURAL NOUN _____

PLURAL NOUN _____

ADJECTIVE _____

PLURAL NOUN _____

NOUN _____

NOUN _____

NOUN _____

NOUN _____

NOUN _____

ADJECTIVE _____

MAD LIBS®
THE EWOKS OF ENDOR

On the forest moon of Endor, there is a group of _____

PLURAL NOUN

called Ewoks. Ewoks are only _____ feet tall, and

NUMBER

they are covered in fur, usually brown or _____.

COLOR

They sometimes have a pattern of _____ or stripes in

PLURAL NOUN

their fur. The Ewoks live in the forest in huts built way up in the

_____. They use _____ tools and weapons

PLURAL NOUN   ADJECTIVE

to hunt, such as spears, slings, and _____. While they

PLURAL NOUN

might look harmless, the Ewoks are more than capable of defending

their _____ from intruders like Imperial troops. They

NOUN

know how to use the resources of the _____ and can use

NOUN

their natural environment to their _____. While they

NOUN

might get distracted if a golden _____ shows up, they

NOUN

remain dedicated to finishing whatever _____ they start.

NOUN

And afterward, they are likely to throw a really _____ party!

ADJECTIVE

MAD LIBS® is fun to play with friends, but you can also play it by yourself! To begin with, DO NOT look at the story on the page below. Fill in the blanks on this page with the words called for. Then, using the words you have selected, fill in the blank spaces in the story.

Now you've created your own hilarious MAD LIBS® game!

MACE WINDU, MASTER JEDI

ADJECTIVE _____

NOUN _____

ADJECTIVE _____

NOUN _____

ADJECTIVE _____

NOUN _____

COLOR _____

ADJECTIVE _____

PLURAL NOUN _____

VERB _____

PLURAL NOUN _____

ADJECTIVE _____

SILLY WORD _____

PLURAL NOUN _____

PLURAL NOUN _____

MAD LIBS®
MACE WINDU, MASTER JEDI

Mace Windu is a/an _____ warrior whose feats
                        ADJECTIVE

are legendary among the Jedi Knights. Mace was one of the

youngest to become a Jedi _____. After that, he
                              NOUN

was appointed to the _____ Council, where
                         ADJECTIVE

he eventually became the _____ leader, second in rank
                              NOUN

only to _____ Master Yoda. He is incredibly gifted as
          ADJECTIVE

a/an _____ and is known on the fields of battle for the
        NOUN

unique flash of his _____ lightsaber. He is also a/an
                        COLOR

_____ strategist. He remains cautious in dangerous
   ADJECTIVE

_____ and is able to predict the way a cunning opponent
   PLURAL NOUN

might _____. Time and again he has rescued his fellow
        VERB

_____ from sticky situations, and he is never afraid
   PLURAL NOUN

to strike against his _____ foes, defeating such fearsome
                         ADJECTIVE

enemies as _____ Fett. His exploits during the Clone
              SILLY WORD

_____ ensure his reputation as one of the greatest Jedi of
   PLURAL NOUN

all _____!
      PLURAL NOUN

From LEGO® *Star Wars*® Mad Libs® • LEGO, the LEGO logo, the Brick configuration and the Minifigure are trademarks of the LEGO Group.
© 2011 The LEGO Group. Copyright © 2011 Lucasfilm Ltd. and ™. All rights reserved. Used under authorization.
Published by Price Stern Sloan, an imprint of Penguin Group (USA) Inc., 345 Hudson Street, New York, NY 10014.

MAD LIBS® is fun to play with friends, but you can also play it by yourself! To begin with, DO NOT look at the story on the page below. Fill in the blanks on this page with the words called for. Then, using the words you have selected, fill in the blank spaces in the story.

Now you've created your own hilarious MAD LIBS® game!

JAR JAR OF OTOH GUNGA

NOUN _____

VERB _____

ADJECTIVE _____

NOUN _____

ADJECTIVE _____

PART OF THE BODY _____

NOUN _____

ADJECTIVE _____

PERSON IN ROOM _____

PLURAL NOUN _____

ADJECTIVE _____

PLURAL NOUN _____

NOUN _____

MAD LIBS®
JAR JAR OF OTOH GUNGA

Jar Jar Binks loved living in his home _____ of Otoh
                                        NOUN
Gunga. Unfortunately, the other Gungans didn't _____
                                                 VERB
Jar Jar very much in return. They were always frustrated with

his _____ ways and didn't like that he was a/an
       ADJECTIVE
_____-maker. Jar Jar could tell that his superiors thought
   NOUN
he was _____, and he would often get back at them by
          ADJECTIVE
sticking out his _____ when they weren't looking.
                  PART OF THE BODY
But Jar Jar tried to be friendly and trusting, especially when he met

a new _____. He was always on the lookout for new
         NOUN
friends, especially since he had lost most of his _____
                                                    ADJECTIVE
ones, with the exception of _____. Jar Jar knew that
                             PERSON IN ROOM
his clumsy ways could get him into a heap of _____,
                                               PLURAL NOUN
but he knew he was good at _____ things, too. In
                            ADJECTIVE
fact, he even helped destroy several _____ in battle.
                                      PLURAL NOUN
Who knows, maybe someday he could even grow up to be a/an

_____!
   NOUN

MAD LIBS® is fun to play with friends, but you can also play it by yourself! To begin with, DO NOT look at the story on the page below. Fill in the blanks on this page with the words called for. Then, using the words you have selected, fill in the blank spaces in the story.

Now you've created your own hilarious MAD LIBS® game!

LIKE FATHER, LIKE SON

NOUN _____

ADJECTIVE _____

SILLY WORD _____

NOUN _____

SAME NOUN _____

NOUN _____

ADJECTIVE _____

NOUN _____

NOUN _____

NOUN _____

ADJECTIVE _____

NOUN _____

PART OF THE BODY _____

ADJECTIVE _____

VERB _____

NOUN _____

LIKE FATHER, LIKE SON

Anakin _____-walker and his son, Luke, have quite a bit in
NOUN

common, even though they might not realize it. Both of them grew

up on the _____ planet of Tatooine. Anakin belonged
ADJECTIVE

to _____ as a/an _____, and Luke sometimes
SILLY WORD   NOUN

felt like a/an _____ when his Uncle Owen made him do
SAME NOUN

his chores around the _____. Obi-Wan Kenobi took an
NOUN

interest in both of them when they were young, teaching them about

the _____ powers of the _____. He even passed
ADJECTIVE   NOUN

Anakin's former light-_____ on to Luke. Both Anakin and
NOUN

Luke were evaluated by Jedi _____ Yoda when they began
NOUN

their apprenticeships. Both men grew to become very _____
ADJECTIVE

pilots and were skilled in the use of the light-_____—but
NOUN

that didn't save either of them from losing a/an _____
PART OF THE BODY

in battle! Eventually, the father and son were able to _____
VERB

together to defeat the emperor and save the galaxy. In the end, the

two of them made a pretty good _____!
NOUN

MAD LIBS® is fun to play with friends, but you can also play it by yourself! To begin with, DO NOT look at the story on the page below. Fill in the blanks on this page with the words called for. Then, using the words you have selected, fill in the blank spaces in the story.

Now you've created your own hilarious MAD LIBS® game!

THE TWO QUEEN AMIDALAS

VERB _____

PART OF THE BODY _____

ADJECTIVE _____

NOUN _____

ADVERB _____

VERB _____

VERB _____

ARTICLE OF CLOTHING _____

ADJECTIVE _____

ARTICLE OF CLOTHING _____

PART OF THE BODY _____

NOUN _____

ADJECTIVE _____

PLURAL NOUN _____

MAD LIBS®
THE TWO QUEEN AMIDALAS

Being a young queen has enough challenges without worrying that

someone might try to _____ you. That's why Padmé
                        VERB

Amidala always had her _____-maiden, Sabé, by her
                        PART OF THE BODY

side. Not only was Sabé a/an _____ companion to
                             ADJECTIVE

Padmé, but in times of _____, she could also protect
                        NOUN

the young queen by taking her place. Sabé was _____
                                              ADVERB

trained on how to _____ and _____ just
                   VERB   VERB

like Padmé, so that no one could tell them apart. When traveling on

dangerous missions, Sabé would don the queen's _____
                                               ARTICLE OF CLOTHING

and apply her _____ makeup, so that everyone
               ADJECTIVE

would believe she was the queen. Padmé would then wear Sabé's

_____ and act as though she was the one serving her
ARTICLE OF CLOTHING

_____-maiden. This was a/an _____
PART OF THE BODY   NOUN

that would trick even the most _____ foes—in fact, even
                                ADJECTIVE

the queen's closest _____ often had no idea which
                     PLURAL NOUN

girl was which!

MAD LIBS® is fun to play with friends, but you can also play it by yourself! To begin with, DO NOT look at the story on the page below. Fill in the blanks on this page with the words called for. Then, using the words you have selected, fill in the blank spaces in the story.

Now you've created your own hilarious MAD LIBS® game!

THE GLEAMING CITY
PLANET OF CORUSCANT

NOUN _____

ADJECTIVE _____

PLURAL NOUN _____

ADJECTIVE _____

NOUN _____

PLURAL NOUN _____

ADJECTIVE _____

NOUN _____

ADJECTIVE _____

ADJECTIVE _____

SILLY WORD _____

PLURAL NOUN _____

PLURAL NOUN _____

OCCUPATION _____

Located in the center of the _____, the planet Coruscant
                              NOUN

is one of the most _____ worlds in the Republic. Once
                  ADJECTIVE

covered in nothing but _____, the entire surface of
                      PLURAL NOUN

the planet now consists of one _____ city. Skyscrapers
                             ADJECTIVE

dominate the view, and while they might look boring during the

day, just wait until _____-time! The gleaming neon
                      NOUN

_____ can be seen from space and draw all kinds
      PLURAL NOUN

of _____ visitors to the city. Home to the Jedi
        ADJECTIVE

Temple and the Palace of the _____, there are other
                         NOUN

sights to see as well. Stop by the _____ Gardens for a
                           ADJECTIVE

peaceful visit or experience the _____ nightlife at the
                        ADJECTIVE

Outlander Club, where you can place bets on Podraces or games

of sabacc and _____. Afterward, you can stop by
               SILLY WORD

Dexter's Diner for a steaming mug of _____ or a bowl
                         PLURAL NOUN

of delicious _____. Just be sure to tip your droid
          PLURAL NOUN

_____, Flo!
   OCCUPATION

MAD LIBS® is fun to play with friends, but you can also play it by yourself! To begin with, DO NOT look at the story on the page below. Fill in the blanks on this page with the words called for. Then, using the words you have selected, fill in the blank spaces in the story.

Now you've created your own hilarious MAD LIBS® game!

DARK VERSUS LIGHT

VERB _____

NOUN _____

SILLY WORD _____

PLURAL NOUN _____

VERB _____

ADJECTIVE _____

ADVERB _____

PLURAL NOUN _____

PERSON IN ROOM _____

VERB _____

ADVERB _____

PLURAL NOUN _____

PLURAL NOUN _____

MAD LIBS
DARK VERSUS LIGHT

Anakin Sky-_____-er was feeling torn. He had been
                VERB

trained in the Force by his Jedi _____, Obi-Wan
                                        NOUN

Kenobi, after tests revealed he had a high _____
                                              SILLY WORD

count, which showed his Force powers. He knew how to use the

Force in matters of _____ and how to defend
                          PLURAL NOUN

himself, but he had been told it was wrong to use the Force to

_____ someone else. But Darth Sidious had begun
        VERB

to show him the _____ power that the dark side of
                      ADJECTIVE

the Force was capable of. If Anakin was feeling anger or sadness,

he could _____ tap into the dark side. He wanted
              ADVERB

to know what _____ the dark side would bring him.
                  PLURAL NOUN

But Anakin wasn't sure if Darth _____ was really
                                    PERSON IN ROOM

his friend or was plotting to _____ him! But still,
                                    VERB

he was _____ tempted. He was curious about what
            ADVERB

_____ he might be able to accomplish, like the ability
    PLURAL NOUN

to shoot bolts of _____ from his fingertips!
                      PLURAL NOUN

MAD LIBS® is fun to play with friends, but you can also play it by yourself! To begin with, DO NOT look at the story on the page below. Fill in the blanks on this page with the words called for. Then, using the words you have selected, fill in the blank spaces in the story.

Now you've created your own hilarious MAD LIBS® game!

LUKE SKYWALKER, MOISTURE FARMER

NOUN _____

PLURAL NOUN _____

PLURAL NOUN _____

NOUN _____

SILLY WORD _____

NOUN _____

NOUN _____

PART OF THE BODY _____

NOUN _____

ADJECTIVE _____

NOUN _____

PLURAL NOUN _____

Luke _____-walker sometimes wondered what his life
        NOUN

might have been like if his uncle Owen hadn't purchased those two

_____, R2-D2 and C-3PO, from the Jawas that day.
     PLURAL NOUN

He might have continued to work with his Uncle Owen and Aunt

Beru and learned to farm _____ on his home planet of
                              PLURAL NOUN

Tatooine. He might have only driven his landspeeder instead of

learning to become an intergalactic _____ pilot. When
                                          NOUN

his friend _____ left to go to the Imperial Academy,
              SILLY WORD

he might have given up and never even made it to Mos Eisley, where

he met his first _____ and witnessed Old Ben use his light-
                     NOUN

_____ to slice someone's _____ off! But
     NOUN   PART OF THE BODY

then he never would have been able to see the _____ or
                                                    NOUN

meet the _____ Princess Leia, who turned out to be not
             ADJECTIVE

only one of his best friends, but also his twin _____!
                                                     NOUN

It really was a lucky thing that the Jawas sold his uncle those

_____ that day.
     PLURAL NOUN

MAD LIBS® is fun to play with friends, but you can also play it by yourself! To begin with, DO NOT look at the story on the page below. Fill in the blanks on this page with the words called for. Then, using the words you have selected, fill in the blank spaces in the story.

Now you've created your own hilarious MAD LIBS® game!

SO YOU WANT
TO BE A STORMTROOPER

ADJECTIVE _____

NOUN _____

NOUN _____

NOUN _____

NOUN _____

NOUN _____

NUMBER _____

PLURAL NOUN _____

ADJECTIVE _____

PLURAL NOUN _____

NOUN _____

NOUN _____

PLURAL NOUN _____

A PLACE _____

NOUN _____

VERB _____

MAD LIBS®
SO YOU WANT
TO BE A STORMTROOPER

The Galactic Empire is always looking for dedicated, _____
ADJECTIVE

recruits to become part of their elite _____ of soldiers
NOUN

known as stormtroopers. Depending on your skills, you might be sent

to learn how to pilot a/an _____ or learn to be part of the
NOUN

crew of an All Terrain Armored _____. You might become
NOUN

a/an _____ trooper and learn how to steer a speeder
NOUN

_____ without running into trees at _____
NOUN   NUMBER

kilometers per hour. You could be sent to an outpost to track

down runaway _____ who might have escaped with
PLURAL NOUN

_____ information or secret _____. Or
ADJECTIVE   PLURAL NOUN

you might get to work on the Death _____, a space
NOUN

station the size of a small _____! If you play your
NOUN

_____ right, a career in (the) _____ could
PLURAL NOUN   A PLACE

be just right for you. Just be sure to keep your _____
NOUN

polished and try not to _____ your new boss because he
VERB

has quite a temper!

This book is published by

PSS!

PRICE STERN SLOAN

whose other splendid titles include

such literary classics as